Seaside Buildings

Paul Humphrey

Photography by Chris Fairclough

W
FRANKLIN WATTS
LONDON · SYDNEY

First published in 2006 by
Franklin Watts
338 Euston Road
London NW1 3BH

Franklin Watts Australia
Hachette Children's Books
Level 17/207 Kent Street
Sydney NSW 2000

ISBN: 0 7496 6604 8 (hbk)
ISBN: 0 7496 6853 9 (pbk)

Dewey classification number: 725

A CIP catalogue record for this book is available
from the British Library.

Planning and production by Discovery Books Limited
Editor: Rachel Tisdale
Designer: Ian Winton
Photography: Chris Fairclough
Series advisors: Diana Bentley MA and Dee Reid MA,
Fellows of Oxford Brookes University

The author, packager and publisher would like to thank the following
people for their participation in this book: Auriel Austin-Baker; Arrandeep Bola
and family; Lucas Tisdale.

Printed in China

Contents

Seaside buildings

At the seaside, there are lots of different buildings.

Places to stay

There are big hotels and small hotels.

The pier

The pier is very long.

There is a helter-skelter at the end.

Helter-skelter

9

The lighthouse

The lighthouse
is tall.

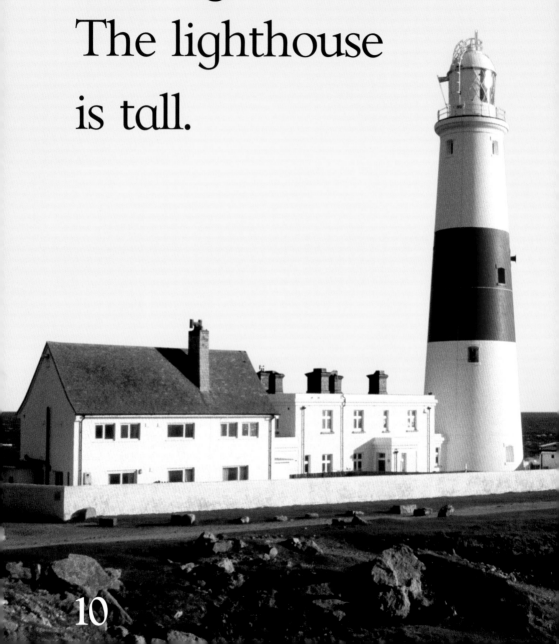

The light warns ships of danger.

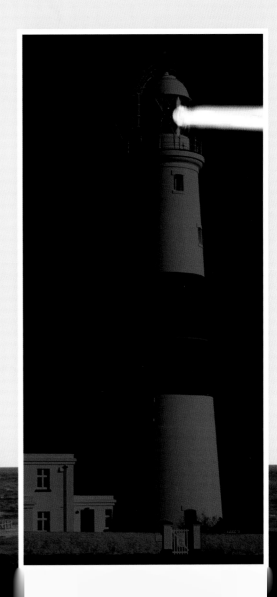

The lifeboat station

This is the lifeboat
station. A lifeboat
is launched if a ship
is in danger.

BEMBRIDGE LIFEBOAT

13

The lifeguard station

Lifeguards watch from the lifeguard station.

They look out for
people in trouble
on the beach or
in the sea.

16

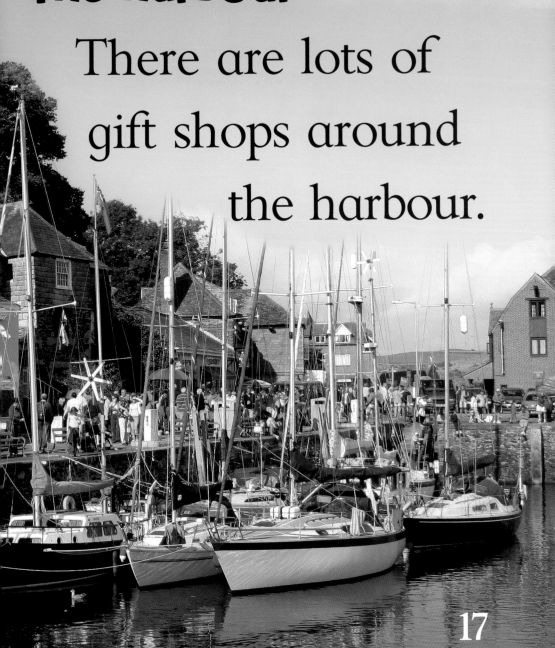

The harbour

There are lots of gift shops around the harbour.

Fish shops

You can buy fish and chips here...

...and shellfish
from this shop.

19

Cafés

People eat and drink outside cafés in the sunshine.

Seaside shops

There are lots of things to buy at the beach shop.

What would you buy?

Word bank

Look back for these words and pictures.

Beach shop

Café

Fish and chips

Harbour

Helter-skelter

Hotel

Lifeboat station

Lifeguard

Lifeguard station

Lighthouse

Pier

Shellfish